THE KITCHEN C

Crab Orchard Ser.     ɪoetry
*Open Competition Award*

# THE

# KITCHEN

# OF

# SMALL

# HOURS

poems by

## DEREK N. OTSUJI

*Crab Orchard Review* &
Southern Illinois University Press
Carbondale

Southern Illinois University Press
www.siupress.com

24 23 22 21    4 3 2 1

*Cover illustration*: abstract blue acrylic painting on canvas (cropped). Adobe Stock (#18687704) by cceliaphoto.

The Crab Orchard Series in Poetry is a joint publishing venture of Southern Illinois University Press and *Crab Orchard Review*. This series has been made possible by the generous support of the Office of the President of Southern Illinois University and the Office of the Vice Chancellor for Academic Affairs and Provost at Southern Illinois University Carbondale.

*Editor of the Crab Orchard Series in Poetry: Allison Joseph*
*Judge for the 2020 Open Competition Award: Brian Turner*
*Jon Tribble, series founder and editor, 1998–2019*

Library of Congress Cataloging-in-Publication Data
Names: Otsuji, Derek N., 1969- author.
Title: The kitchen of small hours / Derek N. Otsuji.
Description: Carbondale : Southern Illinois University Press, [2021] |
    Series: Crab Orchard series in poetry | Summary: "These poems gather
    five generations of family stories about an immigrant experience that
    emerged from the plantation economies of mid-nineteenth-century
    Hawaii"— Provided by publisher.
Identifiers: LCCN 2020055347 (print) | LCCN 2020055348 (ebook) |
    ISBN 9780809338405 (paperback ; recycled paper) |
    ISBN 9780809338412 (ebook)
Subjects: LCSH: Hawaii—Poetry. | LCGFT: Poetry.
Classification: LCC PS3615.T87 K58 2021 (print) | LCC PS3615.T87
    (ebook) | DDC 811/.6—dc23
LC record available at https://lccn.loc.gov/2020055347
LC ebook record available at https://lccn.loc.gov/2020055348

*For my mother and father*

# CONTENTS

Lahaina Obaban Teaches Her Great-Granddaughters about Business and Life     1

The Kitchen of Small Hours     2

A Modern Fairy Tale     3

Music     4

The Road to Kanzaki: A Story about the War as Told by My Aunt Keiko     5

Sadako     7

Death Comes to a Cousin in the Air     8

The Splendor of Laundry     10

Urn     12

Lament for My Father's Sister Whom He Lost in Childhood     13

Shrine     14

How She Loves Music     15

A Brittle Sprig     16

Even the Airborne among Us     17

Redeeming the Cans     18

Last Walk     19

My Mother Revisits Mahelona Hospital, Where Her Mother Had Been Quarantined Fifty Years Ago     20

Lost     22

An Offering with Some Embarrassment and Apologies     23

Returning to My Grandmother's Backyard Orchard the Day after Her Death     24

How to Sell Your Grandmother's House without Remorse     25

The Rabbit in the Moon     26

Three Boys One Fish Two Eyes     28

Among the More Innocent Touristic Amusements of the
     Old Waikiki     29

Bachi Tales     30

Upon Hearing the Old *Advertiser* Building May Have to Make Way
     for New Apartments   31

Getting the Melons to Market     33

Eden     35

Evening Visit     36

Theater of Shadows     37

A Visit to the Hongwanji Temple on the Anniversary of Our
     Grandfather's Death     38

Least Said     40

The Old Flamingo Restaurant     42

The Afternoon We Gathered around a Box of Old Letters and Family
     Photographs Retrieved from the Dust of Oblivion     44

Comfort Food     45

The Reinvention of the American Dream     46

Nostalgia and Memory     48

A Japanese-American Recalls Pearl Harbor Day When He and His
     Teammates Headed to a Football Game in Town Were Fired On
     by a Zero Pilot     49

Apprenticeship     50

Upon First Seeing, Housed at the Bishop Museum, the *Kessho Mawashi*
     Belonging to My Grandfather, Skinny Sumo Wrestler     51

Plantation Town     53

Parable of the Cedars     54

A Marriage in Three Quatrains     55

Industry     56

The Ditch Kids of the Maui Sugar Company     57

The Cane Cutter's Song        58

My Father's Songs        60

Paternal Pedagogy        62

Uncles Talking Story on the Porch        63

On the Recent State of Our Local Economy        64

At the Halfway House        65

Mochitsuki 2009        66

Last Meal        68

First Dream        69


Acknowledgments        73

# THE KITCHEN OF SMALL HOURS

## LAHAINA OBABAN TEACHES HER GREAT-GRANDDAUGHTERS ABOUT BUSINESS AND LIFE

"Women don't drive" was what my husband said.
So I told him, "Teach me to drive, or I'm
leaving you." He relented, once he saw
I meant exactly what I'd said. That's how
*Obaban* became the first woman cab driver
on Maui. You see, I knew the hired cabbies
were cheating us, but I had to prove it
to my husband. I was a quick learner, got
my license and started taxiing. With
the money I brought in just that first day,
it wasn't hard to convince my husband
that the drivers were pocketing the fares.
I got each to confess, then fired them all.
Men are that way. Don't reason, *demonstrate.*

When Aunt Hatsu took a pair of kitchen shears
          to the family album and cut her daughter out
from each picture—soluble life
          suspended in silver tones—the woman knew
what she was doing. Call it love's revenge
          subtracting time from tenderness, a proof
there was no story, just a disturbance,
          swaddled in silence, a stillborn's kept urn.
There was a west-facing wall the late sun
          climbed in afternoons, a day calendar's
torn page discarded with the fading light.
          The paint was the color of nursed remorses,
yellowing then flaking from the bare wall.
          Time's gentle nudges turned the clock hands
to the kitchen of small hours—with its clean
          linoleum floor; white icebox; and, behind
the cabinet door, a cricket kindling—where,
          mixing her days and nights, nights and days,
Hatsu cooked batches of sugar water
          on the stove, boiling, stirring the thickening
syrup of memories in great vats over a blue
          gas flame. When her daughter returned,
Hatsu looked into that dutiful face, like a child
          querying its reflection in a puddle, the soft
lineaments touched by the glamour of recognition
          —familiar and strange, a trick of light.

## A MODERN FAIRY TALE

She didn't want to marry, not at sixteen, not ever—
such music she had heard coming from the piano
of the girl next door, such tall white cakes
baked in the white family's kitchen of the grand

colonial house with its hardwood floors and
parlor rooms. Her misfortune: her beauty, her husband's
status as second son. So she scrubbed her in-laws' floors,
cooked their meat, dined on their charitable crumbs,

while her husband spoke the silent language
of men to their duty and station, and she,
pregnant with their first, spoke the silent language
of the body, refusing to bloom. To the cousin,

she whispered fears that would not quiet, like
a mouse living inside a wall, as she counted
down hours, knowing, not knowing. The child lived
three days. She named her Hatsuko, or *firstborn*.

## MUSIC

Sano Taguchi, at fifteen, eloped with her lover.
And when, at the very door, a mother's tears
could not prevail, the father cooked up his own
scheme to get the contrary child back home.
Those who knew did not speak of what they knew,
while a gabfest of mynah birds gossiped
and gawked. Soon the little family drama
landed in court. Kidnapping charges were
brought against the bride's parents, who kept the girl
hidden. No one could tell the sad bridegroom
"where the cherry blossom of his heart [was]
to be found." So reported the front page
of the *Maui News* June 13, 1919.
Sano Taguchi was my grandmother.

I watch my father's face excavate
old ghosts as his entire past rewrites itself
with each word that my cousin, who'd
discovered the article, reads to us
at the dining room table, where the heart's
sorrows, belatedly guessed, lie in view.
In the story's hot wake we can surmise,
despite the opening hullabaloo, that the
charges against the parents were dropped.
And we know Sano went on to marry, at sixteen,
the man of her parents' choosing. For all
we can tell, she forgave them, accepted
the arrangement of her life, made her bed,
knowing she'd lived to taste such music once.

4

## THE ROAD TO KANZAKI: A STORY ABOUT
## THE WAR AS TOLD BY MY AUNT KEIKO

On the road to Kanzaki, she found an oddly
soothing quality in the ox's clocking trot,
the wood cart's creak and sway as the sun slid

and clouds bloomed with evening's lilac brown.
Then she found herself on the road, alone,
pointed in the direction she should go—

the bombed station, the sea of pleading
eyes, the cool of the river grass, the bus's
swaddled carcass of burning steel giving way

to a moonlit road, a sky shorn of stars
and menaces, as the kind farmer with the
ox cart who had brought her there

had gone as far as he had promised to.
A nursery song remembered from childhood
kept her courage up and the hungry ghosts

at bay, who trailed behind, drawn by the smell
of meat, a slab of rationed beef wrapped
in butcher paper, which she toted in a canvas

satchel slung on her shoulder across her
schoolgirl's uniform. If only she hadn't stopped
at that ration line at the station, but she'd

almost forgotten the taste of beef. Then
the American planes came, rattling the ground
under her feet, the raised glass and concrete

pulled down from around her, revealing
the hellish dream. It all seemed so distant
and strange as the city she now headed to,

under blackout, offered not a single ember,
only the road that shone under that full moon,
lighting her feet the way that they should go.

## SADAKO

A child of the atomic age, she was changed
at the level of the cell, slow stealth of radiation

silently rearranging her DNA. Once news
of leukemia had stilled the room, she put

her hopes in a tradition that said folding
a thousand paper cranes would grant her

a wish. As the end neared, the cranes grew
smaller and smaller. From small and still

smaller squares cut from medicine paper
or the discarded wrappings from gifts of

get well, the angular birds fluttered
at her touch, a white flock off the shore

of a lake. At the last, even her small fingers
proved too indelicate for the exiguous work.

So each crease was put into place by a needle,
pinched with a microsurgeon's precision.

No one knows why she did this, but examining
the tiniest cranes, you can feel the narrowed

attention paid to each fold, the luminous
quality of each whispered crease, the miraculous

accuracy, the disquieting wish,
the child's white secret blandishing an ear.

When your suitcase arrived, postmortem,
courtesy of the airline's delivery boy,
late and soon, we waited a day
to open it and take a look inside,
not out of respect for your privacy,
but out of a kind of stupefaction,
blunt color of nullity left by your
vacated things.
                              Like an old letter
folded, pressed into a book, falling
from turned leaves into the lap
of a reader grown mildly bored
by the material, it was a message
dropped from the afterlife,
even if it was only a suitcase you
packed for the holiday trip home,
and hastily at that, the tossed-in
blouse and jeans skirt and Ts,
(ghosts of old clothes unflown
to winged hangers) tangled with hosiery
(unhoused in scented drawers);
and the gifts it was your custom
to shower family with when you
whirled through town—unlabeled,
left unassigned, in giver-limbo,
with no designated receiver.

But we managed to distribute
the you've-gotta-try-these new
goodies from Trader Joe's. And
the cassette tape of *The Phantom
of the Opera* musical went to

the reticent cousin who loved
theater. As for the pair of oversized
fuzzy plush yellow duck slippers—well,
we tried them on and tramped
around the living room so each
in his/her turn could be Cinderella
of the snuggly shoe (*O, the gagged-up
camp and pomp of it!*), daft undone.

## THE SPLENDOR OF LAUNDRY

In the narrow farmyard, where
  the yellow garden spider has hung
    its web, Grandma is hanging laundry.

White sheets billow and deflate,
  as wooden clothespins are dispatched
    with a swiftness of fingers. In her blue

house gown, she floats through panels
  of light. She might be humming a tune,
    some catch song of childhood carried

across the sea, from the country
  where she was conceived. *Made in
    Japan*, as she liked to say. I watch her

from the window as she moves farther
  down the clothesline and her hands dip
    and flutter along the gentle curve of its

swoop. She is lost in her dream of work,
  where is nothing but sunlight and bleached
    white sheets that belly and slacken like sails,

alternately concealing and revealing her
  to my sight, with the world's bodiless breathing,
    when an abrupt gust wraps a sheet around her

as if she were caught in the sleeve of some
  confiscating angel, whisking her skyward
    wound in the blind flash of an arctic shroud.

But when the wind pulls back, and she
        appears again, just as she was, bathed
                in the impersonal calm and splendor

of laundry, her blurred hands hang
        the final corner of the last white sheet before
                she turns to the house, with that wicker basket,

a gigantic bird's nest, balanced on her hip.

# URN

A copper urn no larger than a jar
that might have held some buttons or some jam
was placed in the family shrine. When I was a child,
it was for me a still object of fear.
I imagined the tiny bones inside
curled up tight like a sleeping baby bird.
Gardenias gathered round it, bloomed, and died.
And each day before the evening meal
a tiny dollop of rice was served up
before it in a tiny gold saucer
afloat like a lily on a gold stem.
The child's name was Hatsuko—three days old.
The firstborn daughter of my grandmother,
cradled in infant sleep, clenched like a tiny
fist of the grief she bore, the death she keeps.

## LAMENT FOR MY FATHER'S SISTER
## WHOM HE LOST IN CHILDHOOD

We never know the last will *be* the last.
At ten, you learned how loved ones walk out
of doors like strangers do, except the heart
chases after, like wind a leaflet's ghost,
as it skitters, scraping a thin music
growing small down a street's gray distances.
Mum went the piano, unspeaking keys,
where her hands, fluffed birds trilling in a bath,
flung up notes clear as water droplets into
the fresh morning air. In the absence of
that song your fingers touch the keys she
touched, a lake breeze rippling the stillness
of a lake reflecting only blankness,
a few clouds, like dreams that have lost their way.

## SHRINE

The room is the quietest in the house.
Grandpa's framed portrait sits still in its place
above gardenias in a porcelain bowl.

He looks out on window-lit emptiness,
indifferent to the blossoming white cloud,
the ripening, oversweet fragrance.

Carnations bring their mute spiced colors;
anthuriums, blood-red hearts, and the air
hangs light with clean scent, but the garden's look

on a day, its soft harvest of flowers,
passes into the grace of ceremony.
Still, there's offering of burnt incense,

brushing his brows with antique silver,
twin scarves of smoke that twine and expire
in unstirred air. Look closer. A perfumed

gesture bids farewell. Then the bell gong sings
its symbolic note of the soul tolled back
through the dim knell of years. The still sound falls,

a communion ensues, the gold Buddha gleams.

## HOW SHE LOVES MUSIC

Such girlish ambitions. My grandmother,
who loves music like a lost childhood,
scales, with the aid of a schoolboy's mnemonic,
the lattice of a treble clef, and from its
looping vine plucks ripe quarter notes,
like grapes grown bluesy with the songs
of autumn rain. As a girl, she lived free
of money, when music lessons were
for girls from moneyed families. Now,
pure melody of the unaccompanied right
hand rings out the old nursed remorses,
cramped penuries since money is at last
enough for an ebony upright (secondhand),
real ivory keys stained the color of tea.

A sprig of cherry blossoms pressed between
the pages of a book—five papery flowers
whose pale pink had faded to the soft brown
of aging letters locked up in a box.

Their discovery was like the discovery
of a note written down and then forgotten,
never intended for anyone's eyes
—just a note to the self to remember

something. No—not a note, but a feeling,
pressed with tender urgency between the leaves
as if to be put in a book—for safekeeping—
as if only in a book it could live.

# EVEN THE AIRBORNE AMONG US

Baby fell out the window up from two stories high.
And where was mother? In bed, asleep,
getting her prescribed bed rest after a year's bout with TB.
So she let the child play on the bed while she slept,
innocent of the invitation awaiting. There was the open
window near the foot of the bed, wearying brightness of
midmorning pouring through, a radiant call to free fall.
And what was baby doing? Fingering a loose
thread in the hand-pieced quilt, the heirloom even then
unraveling, when a blur of colored movement
(red streak of cardinal?) pulled baby's eyes
to the window, its open invitation and promise
of free fall beneath. Tadpole-like, she slipped
headfirst through a clear stream of air.
But soft things fly upward as they fall,
oblivious to their situation's gravity, its stubborn hold
pulling even the airborne among us to earth,
which gathers all in arm to its still center.
The real miracle is that we survive childhood at all.

After she'd lost her daughter to cancer,
she took to crushing aluminum cans
—Shasta, Dr. Pepper, Barq's, Miller Light—
first with her yellow fishcake slippered foot,
then with a real can crusher, wall-mounted,
that she'd bought at the local hardware store.
She'd fill thirty-gallon black garbage bags;
heap them on her Datsun pickup; haul each
rattling payload to the metal scrapyard,
where she got an earnest five cents a pound,
give or take a penny, or sometimes two;
deposited her hard cash earnings in
a modest interest-bearing bank account.
"For my granddaughter's college fund," she said.
At every family party or church luncheon,
she'd ask for the cans. On her morning walks
in the community park, she'd rummage
through the trash bins. Once, an enterprising
hobo encroached on her collection route.
The next day she rose an hour before dawn
just to ensure she'd get to the cans first.
She cashed in cans like this for ten straight years,
as compound interest worked its miracle
or what she understood of redemption,
that the life she had lost (for it is by
grace that we are saved . . .) is bought with a price.

## LAST WALK

He had died suddenly, away from home.
And so she brought his casket to the house
and asked the casket bearers to take him round
the grounds three times. Once for the home he loved;
twice for the orchard's gorgeous gobs of fruit;
three times for the view rolling to the sea,
where on clear days, from the kitchen window,
through phantoms curling off morning coffee,
he could make out an island, mythic, blue,
on the fine horizon's edge, floating free.
The house, the orchard, the unfolding view.
The years it took to make a house a home.
And all the while she walked at casket side,
talking and pointing to the things he loved.

## MY MOTHER REVISITS MAHELONA HOSPITAL, WHERE HER MOTHER HAD BEEN QUARANTINED FIFTY YEARS AGO

Every Sunday that year
we drove all the way
from Kalaheo to Kapa'a Town,
where Mother stayed,
confined to one room.

The roads were bumpy.
I always felt a little nauseous
after the long car ride
that seemed like forever.

Tubercular, prescribed to bed rest, she
was kept from us.

Father would go in
to visit her, alone,
while the twins and I
stood outside in the middle
of the big grassy lawn—waiting,
looking up, up
to the second floor
until she came to the window
and waved at us
from there.

Funny, how the building
seemed so much taller
back then.
        But, of course,
I was a child and everything

looks different to you
as a child.

And maybe, too, it was
that waving at her
through the window there,
up on the second floor,
my mother, whose terrible
love had loomed so close,
at one stroke
seemed so tiny and so far away.

The naked wonder of her own question
takes her aback. Unloosed from the moorings
of place, she blunders about the city,
moving among its buildings
like a child among tall bodies in a crowd,
a shuffle of legs and torsos
rushing blindly, blindingly past. What she clings to
is a name, though what it signifies
she can no longer say, just that
the sound it makes coming out
of her mouth evokes something
comforting, a momentary cloud
of sound her mind inhabits
as if it were a burrow. Each sign,
bathed in alien light, bewilders
in a new direction. She pushes forward,
moving down the narrowing avenue
of her anxiety, from street corner to corner,
searching at each turn for that
flash of the familiar, the healing stab
in the heart she calls home.

## AN OFFERING WITH SOME
## EMBARRASSMENT AND APOLOGIES

These are the last flowers that she will cut
from the raw garden—bird of paradise,

pink cone ginger, the blood-red anthurium
and some green and red ti leaves, out of which

she will make an arrangement to adorn
her mother's grave just as her mother did

for her mother before her. In the vintage jar
(Best Foods), which she scrubs with a scrubber,

resurrecting the clearness, she makes her
arrangement, places it at the gravestone

where lichens nibble at the engraved names,
stands upright to observe her work from

a little distance, then stoops once more to
make some subtle adjustment in each flower

and leaf as the late light touches her face,
like a memory, and she remembers her

mother in these flowers for one last time,
with apologies and regrets, because today

she is selling the house where these once grew,
the house she thought that she would never sell.

## RETURNING TO MY GRANDMOTHER'S BACKYARD
## ORCHARD THE DAY AFTER HER DEATH

There was a way the light appeared at dawn
between the tree of lemons and the tangerines

as if it were a body—and the dew
lit up like coins where its feet touched the grass,

making its presence shine. A golden thumb
pressed into the textured lemons made

lustrous by the uncrushed oil in their skins
and a spider's web strung with water beads,

each spangled with a miniature sun, tented
the branched vacancy as yet unadorned

by the invisible spinnerets of death.
It is this place where the light lives, sunning

on the skins of lemons, that to enter
as I did when a boy I must remove

my shoes, permit the dew to lick my toes,
and step around ever so lightly,

so as not to disturb the slow toad
like a poisonous stone dreaming in the grass.

*Don't grieve*, says the light. Tangerines
like goldfish swim in their groves. *Nothing is lost.*

## HOW TO SELL YOUR GRANDMOTHER'S
## HOUSE WITHOUT REMORSE

Kamaboko slippers tossed in a basket,
one mismatched pair thrown in the tumbled mix.
Green, black, yellow, and brown-blue—the colors
splattered thick and splotched, as on a painter's apron.
You can tell her favorite pair was the yellow.
The sole's soft give, spongy as fishcake loaf,
took the discolored impress of a heel.
Yet each pair made its rounds about the yard
(crunchy heaps of leaves and thorny hedge clippings
from the unruly bougainvillea),
then flopped on board a weekly dump-site trip
in her bright-yellow Datsun pickup truck.
We're cleaning out the house for final sale
when these will go with the rest of the junk.

## THE RABBIT IN THE MOON

I tilted my head back
      and covered my left eye,
            while my father,
index finger to the moon,
      traced the profile of a rabbit,
         a dim figure hidden among
                   lichen splotches
on a disc of bleached bone.

Eager to see
      what I had often heard Grandma say
—that the rabbit is pounding rice cakes
for the celebration of the New Year—
           I followed my father's finger
      with my one open eye and gave close ear
         to the cadenced narration.

Ears, nose, feet,
      the mallet high above
the shoulder,
         the stone bowl full of sweet rice
      coalesced to watercolor shapes
         beneath the touch
    of his finger        and magic placement
      of each word.

The finished image,
      frail and gray,
         was like the shadow cast
           on the paper screen door
         of a Japanese house
               lit softly
from within.

"Can you see it?"
  my father asked, finger pressed
    firm against the moon.

I squinted hard,
  closed my eyes.
    And, as I learned to do with all
  of tradition's distant truths,
    what I could not see,
I believed.

## THREE BOYS ONE FISH TWO EYES

In a cast iron pan Grandma fried whole fish.
The skin crisped up gold brown, with salt and crust.
The eye popped white, a pearl. To eat one just
by myself—me, one fish—was all my wish.
But we were three brothers, and just one plate.
Kneeling on chairs, and ready to "go in,"
we scraped those flanks clean from the head to fin
to tail, till the cooked fish met its bare fate,
clean and lovely, skeletal as a lyre
or a Venus comb with its spokes of bone.
Its popped white eye, how like a pearl it shone!
How we each eyed that pearly eye with desire.
We had to *jan ken po* for that gem's prize:
We were three boys, and one fish with two eyes.

## AMONG THE MORE INNOCENT TOURISTIC
## AMUSEMENTS OF THE OLD WAIKIKI

Freakish as it sounds now, there was a time
when kids dove and swam in the Ala Wai,
launching from the lip of the concrete bridge
that arches over its languishing flow.

My father tells the story of tourists
who came to the bridge to amuse themselves,
tossing dimes into the canal, to watch
as he and bare-skinned cousins, brown as seals,

dove in to chase the winged heads down dim depths
—the flicked coins tumbling, tail over stamped face,
in minted showers, thin slivers of light,
before each plunked disc shivered and then sunk

—dry spectator and scurrying swimmer both
holding in their collective breath until
a clenched fist, hard as American cash,
smashed that cage of glass, and waved like a flag.

Back in the old days sometimes you'd see
a fisherman with a missing hand and know
that it was *bachi*. He'd been blast fishing,
deploying homemade explosives to make
reef waters shiver, bloom—whole shoals belly up
or blank-eyed with the sky, for easy collection.
But as the law failed to catch him, he paid
with the offending hand. That was *bachi*.
A man escaped from OCCC and went
on burglary binge, stealing a woman's jewelry.
Days later there was a fatal car crash
in which the dead driver turned out to be
the very thief, and the woman got her
jewelry back. A boy pranked his little sister,
got her good, detonating cries and screams.
When he bragged all about it to his friend,
the friend said, *Bachi going come around. Watch!*

## UPON HEARING THE OLD *ADVERTISER* BUILDING MAY HAVE TO MAKE WAY FOR NEW APARTMENTS

The historic beaux arts building on South
where the city's original free press was housed,
where off the desks of eager young journalists flew
the first drafts of the island's history—briskly sketched,
provisional—is abandoned now. A graffiti tag
hangs in the square of an awning window. The stucco
is the color of faded dollar bills, and in the ripples
of the Spanish hip-tile roof, small brown house sparrows
nest where the open half-barrel ends meet the building's
eaves. On the street's far side a local construction
crew in neon-yellow-and-orange safety vests has
commenced its trench work, an ocher excavator
digging down to the old water main installed in 1963,
proving history flows beneath the very street even as
progress—in fire protection and upgraded sewage
services to residents celestially housed in faceted
high-rise condos—makes good on its unironic
optimistic promises. The same history housed in
an old communal home, precut, shipped round the Horn,
and assembled by the prayerful hands of missionaries
who found their evangelical dreams tempered by
the natives' easeful grace and faith that raised
the "Stone Church" from the sea, huge slabs hewn
from the sunken coral reef by chisel-bearing divers,
whose pious lungs held out to the last for each saving
miracle of air. The same history flung wide open
as a welcome from the great warrior king, his classic
bronze-cast musculature, his seal-sleek skin draped
ornately in a gilded robe signifying a million gold
feathers plucked from the shy mamo bird, now extinct.
Holding a spear in one hand, he motions magnanimously

with the other, an open gesture of his kingly heart
toward a future he could welcome but not shape.
On the palace lawn a flock of mottled rock doves
startles up, scatters across a blank newsprint sky,
like a story hovering forever above its scrabbled
headlines of a royal wedding, or annexation, or war.

## GETTING THE MELONS TO MARKET

The hot summer long
we loaded
truck beds with

watermelons,
our rough hands
soothed by

the cool green
rivers
in their skins,

then stood guard,
armed with
bamboo poles,

as the cargo
made its way to market
on roads cut

though plantation
settlements. Anything
undefended

was *fair fruit.*
We beat back
swarms

of thieving hands,
playing for the sport
and for keeps,

the occasional casualty—
a tumbled melon
split open

on the road,
   a cracked Buddha
laughing.

EDEN

In October above Grandma's roof,
      avocados darkened, deep
           as the green of Burmese jade.

A reach to mock our grasp,
      a taunt to the aspiring
           touch, they drooped

undisturbed, burdened with ripeness.
      Indoors, saddled with boredom—
           the summer a memory, autumn brooding

above—we waited.
      At a rustling of wind,
           a thud on the roof,

a bump and tumble down
      the slopes of the house, we sprang
           from our seats, flung back the screen door

and rushed outside to fetch the fallen fruit,
      which Grandma would slice
           into two perfect mandolin shells—

half for me, half for my brother,
      she took the seed. We scooped the rinds clean,
           eating even the flesh bruised from the fall

since bruised to our tongues
      wasn't inedible,
           but softened and sweet.

EVENING VISIT

A burning white bulb clouded with small moths
lighted the empty porch and empty chair.
We were expected. Halfway up the path
carved with feet through the cricket-seeded grass
leading to the solitary farmhouse,
we met our grandpa, come down from the fields,
pushing a battered wheelbarrow that creaked
with ball and socket of his failing hip.

He said no word because he'd none to say,
but, reaching down into that battered wheelbarrow,
pulled up a leafy turnip, round, smooth, white
—a plum, like stone, grown in the moon's cold light.
It would be tossed into the pot of stew
Grandma would soon be simmering on the stove.

## THEATER OF SHADOWS

Nights we could not sleep—
        summer insects singing in dry heat,
            short-circuiting the nerves—

Grandma would light a lamp,
        at the center of our narrow room,
            whose conspiracy of light

whispered to the tall blank walls,
        illuminating them suddenly
            like the canvas of a dream.

Between the lamp and wall
        her arthritic wrists grew pliant
            as she molded and cast

improbable animal shapes moving
        on the wordless screen:
            A blackbird, like a mynah, not a crow.

A dark horse's head that could but would not talk.
        An ashen rabbit (her elusive self)
            triggered in snow

that a quivering touch (like death's)
        sent scampering into the wings
            of that little theater of shadows

that eased us into dreams.

## A VISIT TO THE HONGWANJI TEMPLE ON THE ANNIVERSARY OF OUR GRANDFATHER'S DEATH

When the priest talks to us of death and life,
we sit like small children at boarding school.
"Life is like a flower . . ." His voice is cool
as well water, erasing the world of strife.

Beneath the Buddha's feet a lotus blooms.
"This lovely water flower," explains the priest,
"like the meek and humble, grows in the least
promising of places. Yet from a pond's

stagnant depths, where all is murky and cold,
it rises to the surface, blossoms white
and pure, as if burning with inner light,
an emblem of spirit in the turbid world."

The sermon done, the priest withdraws himself
in long ceremonial robes, to chant
a sutra for the dead. All attachment
now falls away, the finite self engulfed

in the infinite, as he steadily intones
tuneless versus that like pure rivers run.
We file, beginning with the eldest son,
before the shrine, the urn that holds his bones,

and then in turn, hands pressed in solemn prayer,
bow and offer incense, burning off in plumes,
while from the singing bowl a bell tone booms
—sound and fragrance purifying the air.

The atmosphere is tuned by singing bronze . . .
Like souls ascending the planes of existence,
curled incense climbs the stairwell of its essence.
The shrine's gold leaf gleams through a veil of gauze.

The sutra dies, the closing knell is struck.
The priest wakes from his trance. With real concern
our aunt inquires about care of Grandpa's urn.
The good priest dispels her fears of bad luck.

Back in the day when streets were named for fish,
at 755 Papio Street
in a fishcake loaf of a Quonset hut

lived husband and wife. They grew carnations
on farmland held in anxious tenancy,
before developers swept the valley.

With them lived their granddaughter, a doe-eyed
Cinderella who, with visiting cousins,
ran barefoot through the fields, her shiny laughter

rattling the banana patch where tall bunches
of green claws grew to measure a child's full height.
When popped blossoms swayed their frilly heads

on wandlike stems, a felicitous trip
of the tongue turned butterflies to flutter-byes.
Finned birds swam about the trees,

and the cousins romped and whirled
about their imaginary kingdom
at the bottom of the sky—life upended

and rearranged so a family might mend
itself as families do, like patchwork,
a grandmother's discreet, deft stitchery

making of the meager materials
of a ruined childhood a fairy tale
complete with a cruel stepmother's bruising

resentments and that hapless father who, whether wittingly or no, had in the end contented himself to look away.

## THE OLD FLAMINGO RESTAURANT

For three weeks, each night we paid a visit
to the hospital room where Grandma
slept out her days, talked through her nights.

I'd flown back from school, mid-term,
to say my goodbyes.

When we gathered at her side and feet,
she told stories about loved ones long dead
as if they still lived next door. Or she'd
muse over far-off, lost relations whose
whereabouts and well-being she worried
to a shiny coin of concern.

But each night with the prompt arrival
of the dinner tray—colorless mechanical soft,
can of Ensure, red Jell-O square—
she'd make an excuse for us to leave
because, by now, she'd reason,
*we must be hungry too.*

Each night for those three weeks
we ate at the old Flamingo Restaurant,
with its salmon-pink facade
and three welcome arrows, bright electric blue,
that arced when lit in sequence,
like a dolphin—in freeze frame—leaping
through the dark, beckoning
hungry diners to come on in and eat.

Sunk in the warm animal coziness
of that worn upholstered booth

in the family's favorite restaurant
where we ate our favorite foods
—for me, breaded beef cutlet with warm
brown gravy over mashed potatoes,
steamed green peas, a freshly buttered roll—
I was a boy again with a boy's hunger.

When I looked up from my food
to wash it down with a gulp of slushy punch,
I saw for the first time that my parents'
faces had grown old.

Against the doctor's prognosis,
Grandma got well. I went back to school.
She lived another seven years.

We never ate at that restaurant again.

Empty now, boarded up, sporting a graffiti tag
like a black eye, the old Flamingo Restaurant
sits on the auction block. But I remember
those three weeks, now years ago
—of family, by illness, brought close,
of the endless talk of loved ones living and dead,
of the punctual arrival of the dinner tray
and the gracious taking leave, as the young
do from the old, and afterwards the food.

## THE AFTERNOON WE GATHERED AROUND A BOX
## OF OLD LETTERS AND FAMILY PHOTOGRAPHS
## RETRIEVED FROM THE DUST OF OBLIVION

After Grandmother died, she visited my cousin
in a dream, instructing her to retrieve a box
from the empty house. Fragile letters winged
with vanished wishes, inquiries after those

who had once waited on their arrival, instructions
and the hurried attendance on mundane things
that time's passing had made quaint. What were
such messages to us now? And photographs

—of faces, some namable, others guessed at,
or provoking wonder and speculation?
But then an aunt, wide eyed, shot a look at
the cousin, whose dead ringer of a doppelganger

stood in a photograph before us, staring out
from the faded past through the wondering eyes
of a child, the pale round face framed
by a pageboy cut, with bangs straight across

the small white brow, and we felt in that instant
how fearsome a thing is that strength in blood.

## COMFORT FOOD

On cold mornings like this, she boiled soup stock
from the little silver anchovies called
*iriko*, sliced winter radish into
translucent half-moons, cut a tofu block
into small marble cubes, and gently mashed
in the miso paste to thicken the broth.
On lucky days there'd be a whole poached egg
in each bowl, green onion for garnishing.
Curling phantoms bloomed in winter's kitchen,
summoning warm bodies round the table,
the legs of wooden chairs scraping linoleum
while cupboard doors on musical hinges
opened, closed and the setting was complete.
It's to this memory the hunger comes home.

# THE REINVENTION OF THE AMERICAN DREAM

*for Kenneth Taba*

Back in your day when there really was
no such thing as a free lunch, you learned
to master hunger with hunger, trading

pocket nickels for books whose inked pages,
dry stand-ins for milk and sandwiches,
you dutifully devoured until your tongue

grew accustomed to the taste of words
all the natives of the place babbled in.
Then war broke out and the smell of your

foreignness got into people's noses.
A beloved character from a looney
cartoon invented a name to nip

at your ankles, pulling the socks off
your bare white heels. So you learned to stiffen,
like the General's statue, green as liberty

and unflinching at the pigeons on his
epaulets. In geography, you found
the colors of the world make it impossible

to tell the good countries from the bad.
Then, moved to music of bombs bursting
—obliterating homeland, language, identity—

you discovered above red noise in that loud
patriotic air, a clearer music, a country of sky,
where great herds of cloud—woolly, thick-

shouldered as the American buffalo—roam
gold prairies, rounded with imaginary
corrals of shining seas . . . blue frontiers.

What is an American? How is a new man made
or remade after the image of his own
invention? A shipyard is bombed and a language,

erased. An old fisherman gets his boat
confiscated. (He'd been ratted on by a neighbor,
a rival, because as a local man liked to say,

*Dah Japanee guy was dah bettah fisherman.*)
A beloved teacher vanishes from under
his pupils' noses, with silence as the only

explanation. When he returns, he mumbles
in broken syllables of the meek. To get to the far
outhouse in a stubbled field, harried *issei* trip

over themselves to prove who is most
patriotic. As evidence they bring family heirlooms
to be heaped and burned, exchanging beauty

for ashes, nostalgia for drunkenness,
feeding high, glamorous flames of self-hate.
In this country of forgetting,

their names remember them, their places
of origin these objects enshrine: lacquer cabinets,
like little black ovens, eating the portable

gods inside and the family registries (such fancy
ideas they'd entertained!) translated
by a leaping tongue, pale curlicue of script.

## A JAPANESE-AMERICAN RECALLS PEARL HARBOR DAY
## WHEN HE AND HIS TEAMMATES HEADED TO A FOOTBALL
## GAME IN TOWN WERE FIRED ON BY A ZERO PILOT

Jostled in back of a hulking pickup,
we'd just cleared Kipapa gulch, headed to
town for the ball game, all eighteen of us,
dressed in red jerseys pulled over squarish
shoulder pads cut from cardboard, when a plane,
seeming to crawl toward us, started shelling.
Flying bullets whizzed above our heads,
pumping the car behind us full of holes.
We hit the ground or, rather, the truck bed.
But who were we kidding? We were sitting
ducks, in RED! From the blood sun on its wings
and sides we knew that the plane was Japanese.
The pilot took just one pass, then buzzed off.
He'd swung low, so low that I saw his face.
And as he passed us overhead or, rather,
as we passed him, we exchanged looks. I/he
were the same in years, give or take one or two.
He had my face, the face of the enemy
I'd soon be turned into. This was the start
of the war that changed others' eyes toward us.
But did I see this? No, I narrowed my eyes
and glowered with the rest, shaking my fist,
cursing as he flew off into history,
my dear suicide already in flames.

## APPRENTICESHIP

Apprenticed to a blacksmith as a boy
—this second son without inheritance—
each day, to clear the clangor from his head,
wipe the forge fire from his eyes, quench his skin,
he'd climb a tree in the cool of the evening
and look in the direction of his home.
At eighteen he'd emigrate, shoe horses
for supervising lunas in the cane, forge
machetes for the field hands, and spangle
Cuban gamecocks with shiny metal spurs
for the sport of the camp Filipinos,
so that his bride was kept from field labor.
Women who toiled alongside their husbands
called her "Okusan," a name for proper wife.

UPON FIRST SEEING, HOUSED AT THE BISHOP
MUSEUM, THE *KESSHO MAWASHI* BELONGING TO
MY GRANDFATHER, SKINNY SUMO WRESTLER


Apart from the family legend
attached to it, the object itself
(the accompanying placard suggests)
is of not inconsequential interest
to local historians, to athletes and their devotees,
belonging as it does to a man
of Japanese descent who straddled—
what would seem to most—the world of sport
at its two extremes,
having been, in his career's short course,
horse jockey and sumo wrestler both.

Look how the curator placed it—
in an empty space,
slightly recessed, in this semidarkened
room so that, lit by the dim light
of the display case where it's housed
behind glass, curious viewers
surround it.

The silk belt opens to a ceremonial apron
on which a dark orange carp,
caught in its heroic climb upriver,
is richly embroidered—the arced body
lifting head and tail
above roiling water, as if
threatened from beneath by
blue devouring fires.

Elegant Chinese characters blazon
the *rikishi's* name in gold thread.
And below, an ornamental band is stitched
with a chain of intertwining flowers
where thick, ropelike tassels fringe the hem.

Each detail celebrates a victory
in the career of that pint-sized wrestler
who leapt into the islands' record books,
and who could topple, handily—as two
uncles can vouch—a Goliath twice his size.

## PLANTATION TOWN

A red dirt road snaking through fields of cane.
Houses, painted green with white trim, marshaled into rows.
A town where sugar, like a decrepit king,
holds sway over a dwindling populace
—diabetic, resolute, and aging.
A squat post office where old mothers bring
mango, bread fruit, pomelo in exchange for
seasonal cards from their smart lucky ones
who moved on to bigger, busier things.
A makeshift fence with termite-eaten posts
strung together by barbless wire, keeping
good neighbors of the stark ethnicities.
Chicken coops marbled with silver-green droppings,
a windblown down feather caught in the hex netting.
The hulking frame of an old GMC
stalled in a patch of golden, sun-bleached weeds.
Fishbone TV antennae propped on roofs
of homes tuned in to other places' news.
Two children running off to somewhere, their high
excited voices ricocheting off silent machinery.
A woman, in the gloaming, crossing barefoot
a boot-scuffed lawn, picking clothespins one
by one, as she gathers in her arms the harvest
of undershirts, trunks, and blue work pants
for each day's labor and leisure through the week.

## PARABLE OF THE CEDARS

At eighteen, you left your childhood village
for the promise of work far away, and in the days
before you departed, not knowing it was
for good, you seeded a field with cedars—
the last planting of your hand, rooting you
to home. Time passed, slow as timber's song.
You forged the tools and implements to cut
another man's cane fields, dreaming of windlight
sifting through the trees whose yearly growth
in your native air redeemed, so you believed,
each year of life you spent away from home.
It was as if toiling on foreign soil
you drew strength from your native ground, your blood
like sap rising through columns of living wood
whose sinews' restrained exuberance stretched
to touch the sun. Time worked its stoic patience
in you, each unspoken hope in slow scrolled
histories recorded by an envious brother's
calculating spite. Fail to send money
home, he wrote, and he would cut the trees down,
terms to which you would submit for years
until the day your wife had had enough,
saying, "I have children, too." So the brother
felled the trees, sold the wood, and, jostling through
the bustling market crowd, lost in evil dreams,
discovered soon, upon returning home,
the empty purse, the ill-gotten money gone.

## A MARRIAGE IN THREE QUATRAINS

He came from the south country, famous for
its island with one blooming volcano,
Saint Xavier and the last samurai,
the giant white radish and sweet potato,

which was the staple food instead of rice.
So once when she, born in "Rice Country," thought
to please her husband with a steaming plateful
of the sweet tuberous roots she had bought

that day at market, without looking up,
he waved the plate away, said to his wife,
"Woman, you can keep your sweet potatoes.
I've had enough sweet potato for life."

# INDUSTRY

By the sweat of your face you laced
with table sugar the languorous teacup hours
of another man's afternoons of leisure

then on leased land imprinted the baked earth
with the narrow furrows of your dreams. Knowing
the way up and the way down to be the same,

you climbed the dizzy ladder of riches
playing the undertaker, cheerful
in the knowledge you'd never lack for clients

dying to cash in. Calloused hand over
patient fist, you bought back lost privileges
that the firstborn, going to pieces,

had divided among three noble vices,
beneficiaries of the family estate,
till, seated at your own table in the manor

you rebuilt plank by stone, you sounded
the clapper of a servant bell, at whose summons
*shoji* doors slid back and a woman servant

appeared—kimonoed, diminutive, rescued
from a desperate fate—holding a lacquer tray
arranged with assorted steaming dishes,

which she laid out before you with ceremonial
exactness, kneeling attentive at your side,
filling your raised tumbler with hot *sake.*

## THE DITCH KIDS OF THE MAUI SUGAR COMPANY

Barred from swimming pools the hot summer long
but loving the delicious cold on our skins,
we dove into ditches dug to irrigate
the same fields where our fathers slogged, under
the supervising eye of a white sun winking
on the blades of their machetes. Of course
there were barbed-wire fences to keep us from ditches,
just as there were codes that banned us from pools
sealed behind an elite sports club's gleaming
walls, a taboo, like a shiny thing, asking
to be smashed.                    Released from sluice gates,
the sloshing water, brown as our arms,
ran down the channels, as we dipped and stroked,
like salmon driven upstream, the russeting
current sliding off flexed shoulder blades
in silted robes as we reached speeds that broke
all barriers and in our homegrown upstart way,
always the outside chance, the dark horse's surge,
we sugar ditch kids, turning laps like verses
of an Olympian ode, plowed that narrow lane
to victory and were crowned aquatic kings.

## THE CANE CUTTER'S SONG

I cut the cane
fields fall
and rise again

Another season
comes and goes
In fields up North
the cane grows

Child and wife
wait my return
I count the days
the fields burn
Black smoke
piles high
I look up
and cannot see the sky

I rise each day
at daybreak
and earn my pay
The sun beats
on my back
My hands and face
are black

A day's work
for the day's bread
a shanty roof
above my head
At night I stretch
in a narrow bed

I was a boy
when I began
Now a man
full grown
I survey fields
where youth
lies mown

## MY FATHER'S SONGS

The songs my father sang
were in another language
lost to me, songs
of an island kingdom
that remember a different sky,
carried from across the sea.

On three unslackened strings
he played those wave-borne songs,
a brown snakeskin *sanshin*
jangling barbaric chords.
Like rain beating rooftops
of corrugated tin,

that battered banjo twanged.
And I tell you, he could sing.
His voice raw with melody
shook the humming air,
made the green valley ring
with greenness. Green longing,

black despair, pale discontent,
and bruised rose-colored
defeat sprang from
three taut strings, a raw ache
plucked from animal's gut
that stretched but did not break.

And his employment, too,
racked on the frame of days,
made its own song—cane cutter
of the strong right arm

that never forgot its cunning.
Some nights, he sang under

a climbing moon. But when
old friends gathered for
holiday—*hekka* bubbling
on the hibachi grate
as little ones swarmed, begging
for crusts of *koge* rice scraped

from the cast-iron pot
—after the meal was done,
the last of the *manju*
and coconut cream cake
polished off, dishes wiped
back to their shelves,

and furniture from
the entertaining room
removed to clear a space
where the women, their
kitchen toil done, could dance
—how he let loose! A torrent

of noisy joy—and brittle feet
remembered steps they danced
on that island kingdom's shore,
where ocean-rolled stones pierced
by fierce whistle calls are
whipped to meringues of wind.

Those autumn evenings, our father home
from his day shift at the old cannery,
the front porch would convert to a study
where my sister and I sat at a table
for nightly lessons in arithmetic.
Multiplication charts written on
yellow legal pads—the neat columns, rows
copied by hand (a precise machinist's),
the same that had kept the cannery humming
for nine years.
           We chanted cadenced sequences
aloud, a recipe of runes mixing rhythm
and memory to produce the miraculous
learning while our father plucked sweet
numbers on his mandolin till we
had gotten the tables by heart. He never
spoke a word about opportunities
he never had, nor recited a single
maxim of what good schooling could do.
But picked harmonics he used to fine-tune
his pitch struck in each a sympathetic
resonance of strings. Beyond the porch light
the cooped chickens clucked and jostled before
resettling into sleep. Moths, pulled into
orbit by the glow, circled the pale bulb,
like hieroglyphs. Crickets under the starred
night sizzled at their strange frequencies
that stirred in us the stranger harmonies.

## UNCLES TALKING STORY ON THE PORCH

Talking story on the cool porch at night,
where the moth flits like a feathery ghost
and the gecko, like a brown god, keeps post
under a naked bulb's yellowy light,
they tell of childhood's wide misadventures
among drainage ditches and brown canals,
rehashed school rivalries, classic fish tales,
war stories and faddish dances, departures,
a miraculous illness, old blood foes,
melodious oldies, and money woes.
Rich with regret, the voices talk all night,
their ample stage: a porch, a yellow light.
Each story says, "I lived, I loved, I lost."
Each sigh recounts, then tallies up the cost.

## ON THE RECENT STATE OF OUR LOCAL ECONOMY

A Portuguese man, speaking a pure musical pidgin,
comes to my father's farm to buy some green onions,
which he will use to make his famous blood sausage.
My father goes to the field to harvest a generous bunch
of the slender blue-green stalks, punched up through
the rich volcanic dirt. When the Portuguese man offers
to pay, my father declines. The Portuguese man insists.
My father waves the money away. They go back and forth
like this a few times in this clash of generous wills until
my father wins out and the Portuguese man walks away
with a chagrined but genuine thank you, though by the look
on his face you can tell he is determined not to be outdone.
My father doesn't see this man again, until months later,
in July, when he shows up at the farm unannounced
with a bucket of Mapulehu mangoes, picked fresh
from the shaggy dooryard tree fronting his house.
The bucket arrives in the same week that my nieces
and nephew are visiting from Utah. They love
mangoes, the taste of local life they left behind for white
desert skies and affordable housing. The Mapulehus
are green red and peach cream gold. Their autumnal
globes hold out a promise of sunlight mellowed
into sugar. My father looks on with pleasure as
his grandkids relish each fleshy slice, and down
the chin of the youngest dribbles a sun drop of juice.

## AT THE HALFWAY HOUSE

He remembers his mother's cooking most
and talks about it often over meals—
aku belly, stewed eggplant, togan soup—
his soft, slow words dreamily conjuring
the rising steam and the summoning smells,
the kitchen warmth. He can't go back home.
"I broke my mother's love for me," he says,
as if it'd been a vessel. In and out
of jail for years, he knows what life is worth,
after he'd almost thrown it all away.
He lives with others not unlike himself,
men bleared with the blue ink of old tattoos.
They sit to share a meal, and offer grace.
He is a boy again with a boy's hunger.

## MOCHITSUKI 2009

The kitchen gossip is brisk and benign—
among the flurry of rice-floured hands,
names of children and absent relatives

are kneaded into the communal dough
—schools, sports, colleges, jobs—weddings and births
soon to come—one child now "secure" because

"employed in a steady government job"
—one "come to no good"—one "soon to deploy"
—and one unfortunate aunt, who "had a

bad fall in her own home" after forty
years of living there without an incident.
The cakes they shape with such talkative hands

are as round as the moon, at least as it's
shaping up to be on coming nights, since
the fisherman's solunar calendar

predicts on New Year's Eve a full moon's rise.
Outside, the men are at their assigned labor
—with mallets fashioned out of lemon trees—

pounding sweet, fresh-steamed rice in a stone bowl,
just as in the moon's depicted fable
in which the mallet-wielding rabbit's worked

his work for centuries and which the clan
now carries on below. Meanwhile, as if
on cue, the governing uncle chimes in

with his one saying never left unsaid:
"Family is like rice; they stick together."
And who can contradict him? They're all here.

The hermit uncle and his estranged wife;
the prodigal cousin without employ;
the spinster aunt—a schoolteacher—who just

"got tenured"; the black-and-white family cat
called "Musubi"—in his accustomed corner
coolly withdrawn and from which vantage point

he takes somewhat indifferent note
of all the chatty, messy goings-on.
Between two aunts an argument (of sorts)

erupts about whether or not something
is "bad luck"—then which is better for frying
eggplant—"cornstarch" or just "plain white flour"?

Spats, superstition, hearsay, wisdom, truth
—it's all kneaded into one. New Year's Eve
the moon will trim and hang its pale lantern,

decorated with curious markings
that are just that and nothing more. And yet,
abstract as black ink brushed on rice paper,

the curious animal-like character
is whatever we believe that we see
or what tradition gives us eyes to see.

## LAST MEAL

On New Year's there are four foods we must eat:
a bowl of clear broth soup with cakes of rice,
five sweet black soybeans, salted herring roe,
and the dry-roasted fish called *tazukuri*.
My aunt prepares each dish as she has done
each year, as her mother did before her,
but which no one since has troubled to learn.
The soup is good fortune. The black beans, health.
The salted herring roe, many offspring.
And the little dry-roasted fish, candied
and sprinkled with toasted sesame seeds,
a strong back that will not bend with age.
She jokes about her slow cooking that gets
slower with each year, apologizes
for this "lonesome talk," then, with a bad hip,
hobbles to the kitchen on uneven steps,
like a parable of good and hard luck.
My brother will not eat his five black beans.
He doesn't like the taste, wrinkles his nose.
It seems like we go through this every year.
My father is chagrined, says, "Eat your beans!"
"Why?" my brother snaps. He hates the taste.
My aunt makes an excuse on his behalf,
in Japanese, something about young ones
nowadays not being used to this kind of food.
Father continues to wheedle and cajole.
"Just five, that's all, and they will bring good health."
But, no, he will not eat his five black beans.
Will not even try. As for the business
about good health, with that he'll take his chances.

FIRST DREAM

For the first dream of the New Year
my uncle pins his hopes on a vision of three things:
Mount Fuji, a hawk, an eggplant of good color.

Seen in sequence, these signal luck
in the coming year. On New Year's Eve, above
the headboard of his bed, he posts a colored print

of all three, exactly as they might appear
in the New Year's dreamer's dreaming head.
"Not one good omen yet!" clucks my aunt.

Here's a man who's seen misfortune.
Retirement savings bilked, investments gone bad,
a daughter snatched by illness prowling

the blood, and a grown son whose mind
took flight in the pious '70s on wings
of angel dust. A wife married to a man of such luck—

what else can she do. It's the first day of 2015.
We're gathered at my uncle's for the year's
first meal. *Ichi Fuji, ni taka, san nasu,*

he repeats, counting down hours
like rosary beads, murmuring the chiming
words like a mantra that opens the cosmic purse,

spilling coins of good fortune, lining
bare pockets of the singing pilgrim with gold.
What he's got instead are goods of more

durable luck, which the coming months
will prove—a knack for loss, contentment in a wife
of fifty years, a mood of rugged cheer.

# ACKNOWLEDGMENTS

Note for the poem "Bachi Tales":
The first bachi tale comes from my uncle. The second tale is adapted from the website Bachi Tales Hawaii. The third tale and concluding quote is taken from the Urban Dictionary.

Poems from this collection have appeared in the following publications:

*Adana*: "My Mother Revisits Mahelona Hospital, Where Her Mother Had Been Quarantined Fifty Years Ago"

*Arc Poetry Journal*: "Redeeming the Cans"

*Arkansas International*: "Among the More Innocent Touristic Amusements of the Old Waikiki"

*Atlanta Review*: "The Cane Cutter's Song"

*Bamboo Ridge*: "A Brittle Sprig," "First Dream," "A Japanese-American Recalls Pearl Harbor Day When He and His Teammates Headed to a Football Game in Town Were Fired On by a Zero Pilot," "The Old Flamingo Restaurant," "Upon Hearing the Old *Advertiser* Building May Have to Make Way for New Apartments," "A Visit to the Hongwanji Temple on the Anniversary of Our Grandfather's Death"

*Bayou Magazine*: "Upon First Seeing, Housed at the Bishop Museum, the *Kessho Mawashi* Belonging to My Grandfather, Skinny Sumo Wrestler"

*Blue Earth Review*: "The Kitchen of Small Hours"

*Briar Cliff Review*: "The Reinvention of the American Dream"

*Burnside Review*: "On the Recent State of Our Local Economy"

*Catamaran*: "Last Meal"

*Chaffin Journal*: "Lost"

*Cloudbank*: "Lament for My Father's Sister Whom He Lost in Childhood"

*Crab Orchard Review*: "Parable of the Cedars," "Shrine"

*descant*: "Theater of Shadows"

*Evening Street Review*: "Mochitsuki 2009"

*Event*: "Even the Airborne among Us," "An Offering with Some Embarrassment and Apologies"

*Existere*: "Least Said"

*Green Hills Literary Lantern*: "Evening Visit"

*Hawaii Review*: "Urn"

*Little Patuxent Review*: "Death Comes to a Cousin in the Air"

*The MacGuffin*: "The Rabbit in the Moon," "Eden," "Uncles Talking Story on the Porch"

*Minetta Review*: "A Marriage in Three Quatrains"

*Missouri Review*: "Apprenticeship" (online featured poem of the week May 21, 2018)

*Ocean State Review*: "Bachi Tales"

*[PANK] Magazine*: "The Road to Kanzaki: A Story about the War as Told by My Aunt Keiko," "Nostalgia and Memory," "Industry"

*Penn Review*: "Paternal Pedagogy"

*Pleiades*: "Lahaina Obaban Teaches Her Great-Granddaughters about Business and Life," "How She Loves Music"

*Puerto del Sol*: "Sadako"

*RHINO*: "Three Boys One Fish Two Eyes"

*San Pedro Review*: "At the Halfway House"

*Sierra Nevada Review*: "Plantation Town"

*Silk Road Review*: "Comfort Food"

*Soundings East*: "Music"

*Spillway*: "How to Sell Your Grandmother's House without Remorse"

*Sycamore Review*: "The Afternoon We Gathered around a Box of Old Letters and Family Photographs Retrieved from the Dust of Oblivion"

*Tahoma Literary Review*: "The Splendor of Laundry"

*Threepenny Review*: "The Ditch Kids of the Maui Sugar Company"

*Typehouse*: "Last Walk," "Returning to My Grandmother's Backyard Orchard the Day after Her Death"

*Wherewithal*: "A Modern Fairy Tale"

Thank you to my Iolani and BYU teachers "Joe" Tsujimoto, Michael LaGory, Lorna Hershinow, Lance Larsen, Susan Elizabeth Howe, and Leslie Norris. Your early encouragement has meant everything to me.

Thank you to Poetry Daily for featuring my work and to the Sewanee Writers' Conference for their generous support.

Thank you to Brian Turner for his belief in this manuscript and to the editors and staff at SIU Press for their expert attention to all that goes into the making of a beautiful book.

And thank you, Mom and Dad, for your faith and unflagging encouragement, especially in the bleak years when it seemed as though the first book might never get written.

# OTHER BOOKS IN THE CRAB ORCHARD SERIES IN POETRY

*The Flesh Between Us*
Tory Adkisson

*Muse*
Susan Aizenberg

*Millennial Teeth*
Dan Albergotti

*Hijra*
Hala Alyan

*Instructions, Abject &*
*Fuming*
Julianna Baggott

*Lizzie Borden in Love:*
*Poems in Women's*
*Voices*
Julianna Baggott

*This Country of*
*Mothers*
Julianna Baggott

*The Black Ocean*
Brian Barker

*Vanishing Acts*
Brian Barker

*Objects of Hunger*
E. C. Belli

*Nostalgia for a World*
*Where We Can Live*
Monica Berlin

*The Sphere of Birds*
Ciaran Berry

*White Summer*
Joelle Biele

*Gold Bee*
Bruce Bond

*Rookery*
Traci Brimhall

*USA-1000*
Sass Brown

*The Gospel according to*
*Wild Indigo*
Cyrus Cassells

*In Search of the Great*
*Dead*
Richard Cecil

*Twenty First Century*
*Blues*
Richard Cecil

*Circle*
Victoria Chang

*Errata*
Lisa Fay Coutley

*Salt Moon*
Noel Crook

*Consolation Miracle*
Chad Davidson

*From the Fire Hills*
Chad Davidson

*The Last Predicta*
Chad Davidson

*Unearth*
Chad Davidson

*Furious Lullaby*
Oliver de la Paz

*Names above Houses*
Oliver de la Paz

*Dots & Dashes*
Jehanne Dubrow

*The Star-Spangled*
*Banner*
Denise Duhamel

*Smith Blue*
Camille T. Dungy

*Seam*
Tarfia Faizullah

*Beautiful Trouble*
Amy Fleury

*Sympathetic Magic*
Amy Fleury

*Egg Island Almanac*
Brendan Galvin

*Soluble Fish*
Mary Jo Firth Gillett

*Pelican Tracks*
Elton Glaser

*Winter Amnesties*
Elton Glaser

*Strange Land*
Todd Hearon

*View from True North*
Sara Henning

*Always Danger*
David Hernandez

*Heavenly Bodies*
Cynthia Huntington

*Terra Nova*
Cynthia Huntington

*Maps for Migrants and*
*Ghosts*
Luisa A. Igloria

*Zion*
TJ Jarrett

*Red Clay Suite*
Honorée Fanonne
Jeffers

*Fabulae*
Joy Katz

*Cinema Muto*
Jesse Lee Kercheval

*Train to Agra*
Vandana Khanna

*The Primitive
Observatory*
Gregory Kimbrell

*If No Moon*
Moira Linehan

*Incarnate Grace*
Moira Linehan

*For Dust Thou Art*
Timothy Liu

*Strange Valentine*
A. Loudermilk

*Dark Alphabet*
Jennifer Maier

*Lacemakers*
Claire McQuerry

*Tongue Lyre*
Tyler Mills

*Oblivio Gate*
Sean Nevin

*Holding Everything
Down*
William Notter

*American Flamingo*
Greg Pape

*Crossroads and Unholy
Water*
Marilene Phipps

*Birthmark*
Jon Pineda

*fieldglass*
Catherine Pond

*No Acute Distress*
Jennifer Richter

*Threshold*
Jennifer Richter

*On the Cusp of a
Dangerous Year*
Lee Ann Roripaugh

*Year of the Snake*
Lee Ann Roripaugh

*Misery Prefigured*
J. Allyn Rosser

*Into Each Room
We Enter without
Knowing*
Charif Shanahan

*In the Absence of Clocks*
Jacob Shores-Arguello

*Glaciology*
Jeffrey Skinner

*Roam*
Susan B. A.
Somers-Willett

*The Laughter of Adam
and Eve*
Jason Sommer

*Hinge*
Molly Spencer

*Huang Po and the
Dimensions of Love*
Wally Swist

*Persephone in America*
Alison Townsend

*Spitting Image*
Kara van de Graaf

*Becoming Ebony*
Patricia Jabbeh Wesley

*Even the Dark*
Leslie Williams

*The River Where You
Forgot My Name*
Corrie Williamson

*All the Great
Territories*
Matthew Wimberley

*Abide*
Jake Adam York

*A Murmuration of
Starlings*
Jake Adam York

*Persons Unknown*
Jake Adam York